NEW YEAR WITH JESUS

A 31-DAY DEVOTIONAL REFLECTING ON NEW
BEGINNINGS AND FRESH STARTS

HOLIDAY CELEBRATION DEVOTIONALS
BOOK 6

PETER DEHAAN

New Year with Jesus: A 31-Day Devotional Reflecting on New Beginnings and Fresh Starts

Copyright © 2026 by Peter DeHaan.

Holiday Celebration Devotionals series, Book 6

Library of Congress Control Number: 2025917928

Published by Rock Rooster Books, Grand Rapids, Michigan

ISBNs:

- 979-8-88809-153-1 (ebook)
- 979-8-88809-154-8 (paperback)
- 979-8-88809-155-5 (hardcover)
- 979-8-88809-156-2 (audiobook)

Credits:

- Developmental editor: Julie Harbison
- Copyeditor: Robyn Mulder
- Cover design: Cassidy Wierks
- Author photo: Chelsie Jensen Photography

To Suzie Rowland

Series by Peter DeHaan

Holiday Celebration Devotionals rejoice in the holidays with Jesus.

40-Day Bible Study Series takes a fresh and practical look into Scripture, book by book.

Bible Character Sketches Series celebrates people in Scripture, from the well-known to the obscure.

Visiting Churches Series takes an in-person look at church practices and traditions to inform and inspire today's followers of Jesus.

Be the first to hear about Peter's new books and receive updates at PeterDeHaan.com/updates.

CONTENTS

THE NEW YEAR AND
NEW BEGINNINGS

As we turn our calendar from December 31 to January 1, our thoughts often turn to a new beginning, to a fresh start. Each new year does that for us. It sharpens our focus on what the next 365 days have to offer.

This helps us understand why many people make New Year's resolutions. They resolve to set behind what was and move toward what will be as they envision a better future for themselves.

Yet deciding to change our lives is just the first step. Next, we must make those changes that we desire. Then the key is maintaining them.

If we are both intentional and consistent about a change, at some point it becomes a habit. Some claim this habit can occur in as little as twenty-one days, while others assert it takes as long as three to six months. The point is that once we repeat our resolution often enough to become a habit, it's much easier to maintain.

Other people greet the new year by setting goals. Though change resolution and goal setting are very similar, the difference is in the implementation. Resolutions result in a day-by-day determination to bring about change. Goal setting envisions the outcome. Goal setters then attempt to move toward that result.

Both change resolution and goal setting can happen at any time during the year, when we most perceive the need. Yet, for many, these most clearly occur on January 1. For some people, this is a New Year's resolution. For others, it is annual goal setting. And some people do neither, merely hoping the new year will be better than the last one.

Regardless of our perspective, as we embrace the new year—or any new beginning throughout our life—this devotional will help us focus our perspective on Jesus and what it means to follow him as his disciple, all while embracing a fresh start.

There is both a practical and a spiritual aspect to making resolutions, setting goals, and embracing the new year. Whichever approach we take, may we do so for our Lord.

This devotional has thirty-one days in it, nicely aligning with the thirty-one days in January. Yet these readings apply equally well any time we want to embrace a new beginning. We can use them when we want to make a needed correction in our life or to celebrate a major milestone. This could include graduating from school, getting married, or having a child. It may mean moving to a different location, starting a new job, or changing churches.

For each transition, we can embrace this devotional as encouragement to move forward into whatever new adventure awaits us.

DAY 1: THE OLD IS GONE
TODAY'S PASSAGE: 2 CORINTHIANS 5:16–20

Focus verse: If anyone is in Christ, the new creation has come: The old has gone, the new is here! (2 Corinthians 5:17)

When we think of a fresh start, of a new beginning, our thoughts should rightly turn to Jesus. Our ultimate fresh start in life begins when we turn to Jesus and follow him as his disciple. With this as our foundational starting point, all our expectations for the new year spring from him.

Through Jesus, a new creation is born within us. Our future, from that moment forward, points us in a new direction. Jesus saves us. In doing so, he makes us right with Father God.

When Jesus forgives us of all the wrong things we have ever done—or will ever do—we become reconciled with God. This allows us to be in relationship with him. What a wonderful gift this is for the created to connect personally with the Creator.

Once we're reconciled to the Father, he gives us a ministry: a reconciliation with others. We share the good news of Jesus with the people we meet. In doing so, we become Jesus's ambassadors, representing him to a world who needs him and what he offers. Then they, too, can be a new creation. Their old self is gone, and a new self emerges.

This all happens when we give our life to Jesus. When we do, he forgives us of all our sins—past, present, and future. There's nothing we need to do to earn this salvation. It's a gift to us. It's offered through God's grace.

When we say yes to following Jesus, our old self is gone. A new self emerges.

This, however, doesn't mean our lives immediately become easy and all our problems evaporate. That's not how following Jesus works. Instead, through Jesus, we embark on a new adventure, moving from our old self to our new self. It's a transition.

So it is when we embrace a new year and a new beginning. May we move forward with Jesus at our side.

Questions: *What does following Jesus mean to us? How can this truth guide us as we move into a new year? What do we think about the old being gone and the new arriving?*

Prayer: Jesus, we thank you for dying to save us and making us right with Father God. Through you, we are a new creation. Because of you, we move away from who we are and move toward something better.

If you haven't yet decided to follow Jesus, will you make that decision today? See Luke 9:23.

DAY 2: FORGET THE PAST

TODAY'S PASSAGE: ISAIAH 43:18–19

Focus verse: "Forget the former things; do not dwell on the past." (Isaiah 43:18)

I saiah tells the people to forget what was, to not fixate on what has already happened. But these aren't just Isaiah's words. The prophet quotes the very words of God.

We are to focus on the future and not the past. Through this verse we find encouragement to forget what was and look forward to what can be. To anticipate what God will do for us and through us. As Isaiah writes elsewhere, God is doing a new thing (Isaiah 42:9).

Perhaps the single biggest obstacle that prevents

us from moving toward a better tomorrow is when our past weighs us down. Memories of what we have done and the remorse that surrounds our missteps can serve as an anchor to keep us fixated on our shame.

As long as we have an anchor that holds us to what we have done, we will never move forward to embrace the new beginning God wants us to have. We must either hoist our anchor or sever its chains if we have any hope of breaking free and moving forward. If we don't, we'll remain tethered to our past. This will prevent us from seeing a better tomorrow.

Though it's critical to not let former mistakes hold us back, it may be unwise to erase them completely from our memory. As the saying goes, if we don't learn from history, we're doomed to repeat it. Stated another way, if we don't learn from the pain our sins produced, we're apt to repeat that same mistake.

This means we can use our past to inform our future, while at the same time not allowing that history to keep us stagnant and bind us to a place we want to move away from.

We can seek a trusted friend to help us navigate this challenge of forgetting the past. We can also receive help from a minister or Bible-believing counselor.

Yet a better place to start is with Jesus. We can give him our past and ask him to guide us in moving forward. Then we can seek the Holy Spirit to direct us every step of the way.

Questions: *What in our past holds us back from our future? What steps should we take to forget the former things that hold us captive? How can we turn this over to our Lord?*

Prayer: Father God, we turn our past over to you —along with our shame, remorse, and guilt— mindful that Jesus has already forgiven it. Because of his amazing gift to us, let us remember that our sins remain in the past—and may we leave them there. Help us turn to the Holy Spirit to guide us in moving forward to embrace the new beginning you want us to have.

DAY 3: A NEW HEART

TODAY'S PASSAGE: EZEKIEL 36:24–32

Focus verse: I will give you a new heart and put a new spirit in you. (Ezekiel 36:26)

The prophet Ezekiel speaks to the people of Judah. They're in turmoil. Their situation is bleak, and their future doesn't look any better. Hopeless might best describe it. Yet today we always have a reason to hope through Jesus.

Amid their distress, God gives them a promise, which Ezekiel records for us to read today. This repeats a pledge the Lord had already made once before (Ezekiel 18:31).

In both passages, God says he will give his

people a new heart; he will put a new spirit in them. This idea of a new heart and a new spirit symbolizes a fresh start in their relationship with God.

Though this promise applies directly to the people of Judah, we're not wrong to claim it as a promise to us today.

God will take away our hard heart—a heart of stone—and give us a new heart of flesh. A heart of stone is inanimate; it feels nothing. Contrast this to a heart of flesh. It's alive; it feels everything. That's what God wants for us, and he'll give it to us.

But there's more. God will also give us a new spirit. This is a fresh perspective—God's perspective. We can see this promise of a new spirit fulfilled in grand fashion at Pentecost when God sends the Holy Spirit to live in and guide Jesus's followers. The Holy Spirit settles on them like tongues of fire and gives them supernatural abilities (Acts 2:1–12).

Everyone who follows Jesus has the same Holy Spirit living in them today.

As we look forward to a new beginning, may we receive from God a heart of flesh and move forward with it.

May we likewise advance with a new spirit—the Holy Spirit. He will guide us in all that we do.

Questions*: Do we have a heart of stone or a heart of flesh? If our heart is dead, what should we do? As followers of Jesus, we have the Holy Spirit in us, but do we listen to what he tells us to do?*

Prayer: Holy Spirit, may we turn to you to receive what we need to move forward in embracing the new year and our fresh start. May we listen to what you say, hear what you reveal to us, and obey your instructions. Bless us as we do.

DAY 4: CROWNED WITH BOUNTY

TODAY'S PASSAGE: PSALM 65:9–13

Focus verse: You crown the year with your bounty, and your carts overflow with abundance. (Psalm 65:11)

King David sings a song of praise to the Lord. It proclaims God as one who answers the prayers of those who come to him. He blesses them and provides for them.

In David's day, the people lived in an agrarian society. They planted crops and harvested the produce. They maintained herds of animals that provided milk and meat to feed them. David's psalm reflects God's provisions to sustain them.

In today's passage, we see God cares for the

land and waters it. He enriches it with abundant results. The crops grow and produce grain. He blesses the fields. He crowns the year with his bounty, and the harvest overflows abundantly. Flocks frolic in the meadows; the valleys wear grain as their mantle. They shout for joy and sing praises to God.

Though some of us today still directly depend on the land for our daily sustenance, most of us are a step or two removed from planting and harvesting crops, as well as raising livestock to feed us.

This, however, doesn't mean that God won't crown our year with bounty, that we won't overflow with abundance. It's just that the crown of our year's bounty and abundance may look different.

The crown of our year may be a new job, a fresh start on life, or our Lord's favor on what we do. We might see the crown of our new year come as a new relationship, material blessings, or spiritual growth.

Though the meaning of the phrase *crown the year with your bounty* will mean different things to each person, the one thing in common is that it comes from God.

We can praise him for it. We can thank him— and we should.

Through him, our carts can overflow with abundance.

How encouraging this is to know that when we come to God, he answers our prayers, blesses us, and provides for us.

Questions: *What does our crown of the year look like? Do we see our life overflowing with God's abundance? If we only see our life as lacking, how should we react?*

Prayer: We praise you, Heavenly Father, for your provisions, for carts overflowing with abundance. Open our eyes to see how you will crown our year with bounty. May we receive what you offer with thanksgiving and praise. We thank you, Lord, for who you are and all that you do.

DAY 5: PLANS TO PROSPER
TODAY'S PASSAGE: JEREMIAH 29:10–13

Focus verse: "For I know the plans I have for you," declares the Lord, "plans to prosper you and not to harm you, plans to give you hope and a future." (Jeremiah 29:11)

The prophet Jeremiah—a contemporary of Ezekiel—prophesies to the people of Judah who have turned their backs on God and are undergoing punishment for their rebellion. This is a dire time for them (see Day 3).

Though their enemy has conquered their nation and deported many of the people, there is a reason for hope. This hope comes from God. For apart from him, there's no realistic reason for the people to have any expectations whatsoever.

Recording the words of God, Jeremiah proclaims that after seventy years of captivity in Babylon, God will rescue them. He will come to them and bring them back to their homeland. It's his promise to his people. This is one of the Bible's few prophecies with a precise timeline. And history reveals the accuracy of Jeremiah's seventy-year prediction.

God continues his promise by giving the people one of the most encouraging declarations in the Old Testament prophetic books. He says, "I have plans for you. Count on it. I want to see you prosper and don't want you to suffer harm. I want to give you hope and provide you with a better future."

The context of this prophecy applies directly to the exiled people from the former nation of Judah. Yet, if God had plans for the people then, he surely has plans for us now. This verse assures those from long ago—and us today—that God has good plans for our future. This gives us hope for a prosperous year and a fresh start.

Yet after seventy years, when God orchestrates the opportunity for the people to return to their homeland, not everyone leaves. Some stay in

Babylon. They're content there. Or they just don't want to move. Regardless, they miss out on the full plans God has for them.

From this, we can learn an important lesson.

When God has plans for us, we need to do our part to receive them. If we sit back and do nothing, we risk missing out on what God offers. We may not receive his best. We could end up with something less than what he wants to give us.

To realize the bounty of God's plans for us, we must remain poised to do our part to receive them.

Questions: *Do we believe God has plans to prosper us and give us a better future? To realize all that his plans offer us, what must we do to cooperate with him?*

Prayer: Lord, we praise you for the plans you have for us. We believe you want to prosper us and not harm us. We trust you and hope for a better tomorrow. Show us what we must do to receive all that you want to give us. Thank you.

DAY 6: MAKE EACH DAY COUNT

TODAY'S PASSAGE: PSALM 90

Focus verse: Teach us to number our days, that we may gain a heart of wisdom. (Psalm 90:12)

Did you know Moses wrote one of the psalms? The man who led God's people out from Egypt to the promised land also penned Psalm 90. (We find three more of Moses's songs in Deuteronomy 27:15–26, Deuteronomy 32:1–43, and Deuteronomy 33:2–5.)

In contrast to the more upbeat content from his three songs in Deuteronomy, Moses's words recorded for us in Psalm 90 are less positive and more apt to produce discouragement. Moses's psalm talks of God's power and our frailty. It mentions God's anger toward his rebellious children. (Though Moses has the descendants of Abraham in mind, are we any different today?) Next Moses reminds us of God's infinite existence and our finite life.

Moses's prayer to God, at the two-thirds mark in this psalm, is that God will teach us to count our days. Doing so will give us wisdom.

Whereas 18-year-olds look to the future as a nearly endless opportunity, 80-year-olds often focus on the limited time before them. Yet each should number their days, for no one knows if this year will be our last. In fact, no one knows if today will be our last day.

When Moses asks God to teach us to number our days, it helps us understand the brevity of life. It's a reminder to live each day wisely. Don't squander another year—or another day. When we make the most of each day God gives us, we will find joy that can only come from him.

Moses ends the song with a prayerful request. He asks that God's favor will rest upon us. That he will establish the work of our hands. So that we don't miss it, Moses repeats his last request: that God will establish the work of our hands.

What does *establish the work of our hands* mean? It

implies that God will confirm our work, bless our labor, and grant us success. May it be so.

As we move forward into a new year or a new beginning, let us do so being fully aware that the future is unknown. We don't know how much time we have left. And too many people don't realize this truth until they have foolishly squandered too many of their allotted days.

Therefore, we should make each day count. We should seek God's favor and trust him to establish the work of our hands.

Let us seek to do so, starting today.

Questions: *What is our attitude toward the number of days we have left? Is there anything about our perspective that should change? What have we been putting off that we should do today?*

Prayer: Lord, may we rightfully number our days and use the wisdom that results from it to live for your honor. Show us how to live each day—and each year—to the fullest. May we not squander another precious moment. We ask this in Jesus's name. Amen.

DAY 7: NEW EVERY MORNING
TODAY'S PASSAGE: LAMENTATIONS 3:22–27

Focus verse: His compassions never fail. They are new every morning. (Lamentations 3:22–23)

The five-chapter book of Lamentations is a series of five laments often attributed to the prophet Jeremiah. A lament expresses grief, mourning, or deep regret.

As such, we expect the book of Lamentations to be a series of negative refrains that express unquenchable sorrow. In short, we expect it to be a downer. It's no wonder many people skip reading Lamentations.

Yet these passages are not void of hope. We can also find encouragement from within. In his third lament, the writer states that God's compassion toward us is endless. Because of his faithfulness, each day emerges as a new one—a fresh opportunity. This passage reminds us of God's steadfast love, immense mercy, and endless grace, which he renews to us each morning.

As we move forward to embrace our new beginning or fresh start through Jesus, we need to be realistic and know that not every day will move us steadily toward the outcome we seek.

Though we could focus on one bad day and let it breed a series of bad days to follow, we're better off to push aside what was (see Day 2: Forget the Past). That way we can better embrace God's blessings that the new day offers us.

When discouragement befalls us on our march to take hold of the future we seek, may we find encouragement in God's love for us. He loves us so much—endlessly so. Our troubles will never consume us; he won't let them. Instead, he will provide, and we will move forward. Through God, we can progress from one bad day that didn't go as expected to start afresh in the morning with great expectation.

God's provision to us will help us move forward.

Questions: *How do we react when our day didn't go as we wanted? Do we lament what was or celebrate what will be? Jesus offers us grace and mercy, but do we offer it to ourselves? What should we do to better embrace God's endless compassion and love?*

Prayer: Jesus, we thank you for loving us and dying in our stead to reconcile us with Papa. You offer us grace and mercy. May we likewise extend grace and mercy to ourselves on those days that fall short of expectation. Give us the strength to embrace each day as a gift from you. May it be so.

DAY 8: TRUST IN THE LORD
TODAY'S PASSAGE: PROVERBS 3:1–12

Focus verse: Trust in the LORD with all your heart
and lean not on your own understanding; in all
your ways submit to him, and he will make your
paths straight. (Proverbs 3:5–6)

Solomon wrote much of the book of Proverbs. He opens with instructions to his son, using the phrase *my son*. But we don't know which son he writes to. Perhaps he hopes each of his boys will receive this as a personal message just to himself.

Regardless, Solomon's message to his son is one we can also receive as God's message to us as his sons and daughters. May we welcome Solomon's wisdom and apply it to our lives as we move to embrace the days before us.

In one of the more popular passages from the book of Proverbs, Solomon tells his son—and us— to trust in God, don't rely on ourselves, but to submit to him. The result is a straight path.

Though we're quick to claim the promise of a straight path, we must not set aside the three prerequisites that precede the promise of a stream-lined quest.

First is completely trusting in God. This isn't just to trust him a little or to trust him partially. It's trusting him with our whole heart. The opposite is placing our trust in ourselves. May we never do that.

Next is not relying on our own abilities. We shouldn't depend on our own intellect and learning. Instead, we should learn to lean on him. Yes, God made us with certain skills and talents. We should thank him for these and use them. Yet we should never put our confidence in our own capabilities.

Third is to submit to him. Specifically, we're to surrender our ways to our Lord. This suggests we should give our plans to him—be it a resolution, a goal, or a new beginning. We should yield our will to him. In all that we do, we should defer to God to do his will and bring honor to his name.

When we do these three things, he will guide us as we move forward. He will give us a straight path to reach our destination. It won't be a winding route that lengthens our journey, encounters detours, or makes us wonder when we'll reach our goal. Instead, he gives us a straight path.

In short, we need to trust God's plan and seek his guidance in all that we do. Any other approach might cause futility or produce failure.

Questions: *How well do we do at trusting God, relying on him, and submitting to him? When we encounter roadblocks on our journey through life, do we blame God or look to see where we might have fallen short?*

Prayer: Heavenly Father, may we trust you with our whole heart. Let us not depend on ourselves but rely on you. Encourage us to submit to you in all that we do. We thank you for making our paths straight and moving us toward our destination.

DAY 9: REJOICE IN THE LORD
TODAY'S PASSAGE: PHILIPPIANS 4:4–9

Focus verse: Rejoice in the Lord always. I will say it again: Rejoice! (Philippians 4:4)

As we embark on something new, we do so with anticipation of what awaits us. This can range from unrestrained excitement to a committed resolve. For this, we have much reason to celebrate. We rejoice in the Lord. I say it again: rejoice!

Yet, as we move forward, our enthusiasm will inevitably wane. What will we do when this occurs? We will rejoice in the Lord.

We may not feel like rejoicing amid moments of difficulty, but we should do so anyway. Paul writes to rejoice in God always. Not just when things are going well, but also when things aren't going so great. What should our response be? Rejoice!

But the instruction to rejoice is just the first of many of Paul's final instructions to the Philippian church.

He continues by saying to not be anxious about anything. Stated another way, we are to be anxious about nothing. That is, to worry over no thing. How do we do this?

We pray. Prayer is key. We'll cover this more deeply in Day 14 when we talk about presenting our requests to God.

When we banish anxiousness and present it to God in prayer, his peace will come upon us. This peace makes no sense in the tangible world. It's a supernatural contentment that we cannot under-stand. God's peace will protect our hearts and our thoughts, keeping them focused on Jesus. This aptly directs us and keeps us properly anchored as we move forward into our new beginning.

Paul concludes by telling the brothers and sisters in Philippi to think about whatever is true, noble, right, pure, lovely, and admirable—anything that's excellent and praiseworthy. May we let Paul's teaching frame our attitude and guide our thoughts as we embrace our new beginning.

As we do what Paul instructs, a natural byproduct will be to rejoice in the Lord. I say it again: rejoice!

Questions: *How well do we do at rejoicing in the Lord in every situation? To banish anxiousness from our lives, are we able to give our worries to God? If we don't have God's peace in our lives, what should we do?*

Prayer: Jesus, may we receive Papa's peace to guard our hearts and our minds in you. Show us how to dwell on whatever is true, noble, right, pure, lovely, admirable, excellent, and praiseworthy.

DAY 10: CRIES OF JOY
TODAY'S PASSAGE: PSALM 47:1–9

Focus verse: Clap your hands, all you nations; shout to God with cries of joy. (Psalm 47:1)

Yesterday's reading encouraged us to rejoice in the Lord always. Today's passage comes from the Old Testament book of Psalms, and it's written by the Sons of Korah. The text gives us an idea of one way to rejoice. It's a physical display of worship.

Clap your hands. It's like giving God applause.

The psalmists envision all nations throughout the entire world clapping their hands in praise to God. I've experienced a glimpse of this at church services. Perhaps you have as well. The congregation applauds God for who he is and what he has done. They clap their hands. I've even heard ministers instruct attendees to give God a clap offering. I wonder if today's focus verse is the impetus for that instruction.

Our celebration of the Lord God continues. Following our clapping is shouting to God with cries of joy. Since the primary definition of the word cry is to shed tears, we may not immediately connect cries with joy.

Yet secondary meanings of *cry* are to call loudly, make a public proclamation, and give an utterance of emotion. To get a glimpse of this, imagine being in the crowd celebrating a come-from-behind win of your favorite sports team—along with tens of thousands of other fans. It could be a buzzer-beating basket, a walk-off home run, or the winning touchdown as a game clock winds down. The result is shouting cries of joy.

But instead of doing it for a sports team that gave us an exciting game to watch, we do this for our Creator who gave us a wondrous life to live, for making us and saving us. He is all powerful and most worthy of our praise. Psalm 47 reflects this.

It proclaims God Most High as awesome, the great King over the entire world. He conquers our enemies and gives us an inheritance. He reigns over everyone. And people assemble before him. They exalt him.

In short, this psalm calls us to celebrate with joy and give praise to God for who he is and what he is doing. This should mightily motivate us as we embark on our new beginning and incite us to action as we start our life afresh.

But what if we don't feel like clapping our hands or shouting with cries of joy? We do it anyway. Though our feelings are fickle, God never changes. He deserves our joy and our praise, whether or not we feel like it.

When we walk with Jesus, we're on the winning team. With him on our side, we will prevail. This truth should fill us with joy and erupt in exuberant worship.

Questions: *How can we best praise God? In what ways has our joy to our Lord manifested itself? When we don't feel like clapping and shouting to the Almighty, do we do it anyway?*

Prayer: Jesus, may we be ever mindful to praise you. We have put our faith in you to save us. Show us how to likewise put our confidence in you as we embark on our new beginning.

DAY 11: SEEK FIRST

TODAY'S PASSAGE: MATTHEW 6:25–34

Focus verse: "But seek first his kingdom and his righteousness, and all these things will be given to you as well." (Matthew 6:33)

As we go through life, it's common for many to worry. They fret about today, and they fret about tomorrow. The issues of life—ranging from matters of survival to trivial concerns—confront them and weigh them down. At a basic level, they agonize over having the basic requirements of life: food, drink, and clothing.

Jesus acknowledges this reality in his lengthy teaching, often called the Sermon on the Mount. But recognizing our tendency to worry doesn't validate it. Instead, Jesus tells his audience then—and us now—to not worry.

Instead, we are to seek first his kingdom and his righteousness. Then the rest will fall into place.

To seek God's kingdom is to turn our attention to him. We make him our priority. This means we serve him and his kingdom. We seek ways to grow his realm. And we invite others to be part of his domain.

But seeking first his kingdom is only part one of Jesus's essential instruction. The second part is to seek God's righteousness.

To seek God's righteousness is to reorder our life to right living. It means we align our actions and our attitudes with what we read about in the Bible. In short, we obey God and do what he says.

Yet our pursuit of righteousness isn't to earn God's favor, any more than we need to earn our salvation. Our pursuit of righteousness is in response to what Jesus has done for us. Our right living is a way of thanking Jesus for saving us and working in our lives. It's a way to show him just how serious we are in our walk with him.

This is what Jesus means when he says we're to first seek God's kingdom and his righteousness. It's the antidote to worry.

When we embark on a new beginning, we may fixate on it with dogged determination. We set aside all that will impede us from realizing our resolution, goal, or expectation for a better tomorrow.

Though there's benefit in not letting distractions derail us or sidetrack us from reaching our desired outcome, it's critical that we don't miss Jesus's command to seek God's kingdom and righteousness above all else.

As we do this, we'll then receive the secondary things we need. Jesus says so.

Questions: *Do we worry about the future or trust God with it? Do we truly seek God's kingdom first? How well are we doing at living our lives with righteous intention?*

Prayer: Jesus, may we take seriously and diligently your instruction to put God first, seeking both his kingdom and his righteousness above all else. Through you, may we cast worry aside and place our future in our Father's hands.

DAY 12: HOPE IN THE LORD
TODAY'S PASSAGE: ISAIAH 40:28–31

Focus verse: Those who hope in the Lᴏʀᴅ will renew their strength. They will soar on wings like eagles; they will run and not grow weary, they will walk and not be faint. (Isaiah 40:31)

D o you ever become discouraged? Have you ever thought about giving up, that the effort you're putting forth doesn't seem to move you toward the outcome you seek?

I suspect we all face discouragement from time to time. We can get overwhelmed by the hurdles before us. This is especially true as we embrace a fresh start. The thing we resolved to do is harder than we imagined. Our goal once felt so clear, but now it seems little more than an unrealistic dream. The allure of a new start has lost its appeal. Maybe what was isn't so bad after all.

When these challenges confront us, we have three options. We can give up. We can push through on our own strength. Or we can place our hope in our Lord. May we choose this last option.

Today's verse assures us that when we place our hope in God, we will have renewed strength and energy. God can counter our discouragement. He will restore us and give us his strength. Then we will soar like eagles. We will run the race before us but not get tired. Even when we walk, we will persevere and not faint under the blazing sun.

Why?

Because we look to God and keep our eyes focused on him. We have placed our hope in our Lord. When we do this, we will realize these outcomes. In a figurative sense, we will soar in the heavens. We will run as much as we need to. And we will walk and not be overcome.

Yet the alternatives—to give up or to push through using our own abilities—may be our default response to discouragement. How much better and how much easier it will be when we place our hope in our Lord.

Questions: *What is our default response when we face discouragement? What does it mean to place our hope in God? Despite God's promise to us, why do we sometimes bungle through on our own when we could soar with eagles?*

Prayer: Lord Jesus, we have placed our hope in you for our salvation. Likewise, show us how to place our hope in you for our daily lives. As we move forward into our new beginning, may we place our hope in you.

DAY 13: PUT OFF YOUR OLD SELF
TODAY'S PASSAGE: EPHESIANS 4:17–32

Focus verse: You were taught . . . to put off your old self . . . and to put on the new self, created to be like God in true righteousness and holiness.
(Ephesians 4:22 and 24)

In Paul's letter to the Ephesian church, he instructs them in how to live for Jesus. We read this in today's passage. Paul talks about getting rid of the old self and embracing a new self.

The context is moving into our salvation through Jesus. In this manner, we shift from our old way of living, recognizing that sinful desires have corrupted us. Instead, we move forward with a new attitude, keeping our minds set on Jesus. We focus on a new self as created by God to be righteous and holy.

If you're beginning your new life as Jesus's follower, this passage contains a wealth of applicable encouragement and instructions. It informs you what to do to move from your old sinful self to embrace your new righteousness through Jesus.

Regardless of where we are in our walk with Jesus, this is the primary context of this passage. Yet we can also find encouragement in Paul's instructions and apply it to any new beginning we embark upon—providing, of course, that we do so with Jesus.

We need to do things in a new way through Jesus. We can't continue living the way we always have and expect a different outcome. As a result, we set aside the things that hold us back, such as sensual pursuits, indulging in impurity, and being motivated by greed. These come from following our fleshly desires.

Therefore, we must get rid of falsehood, thievery, unwholesome talk, bitterness, rage, anger, brawling, slander, and malice. These traits have no place for us as followers of Jesus and no place as we move forward to embrace a new tomorrow.

Instead, we need to adopt a new attitude and

New Year with Jesus

renew our minds in Jesus. We need to put on our new self, which has God-honoring righteousness and holiness. We must speak truth and build others up. And we must be kind to all, showing them compassion. Most importantly, we must forgive everyone, just as Jesus forgave us.

We must put off our old self and put on our new self through Jesus. We do this day by day as we move closer to him.

This is the mindset and the framework that help us move into our new beginning.

Questions: *What parts of our old self are we clinging to that we must leave behind? What characteristics of our new self do we need to be more intentional about pursuing? As we seek our new beginning, what do we need to set aside and what do we need to embrace?*

Prayer: Holy Spirit, reveal to us elements of our old self that we need to get rid of. Show us how to move forward to embrace the new life you want to give us.

DAY 14: PRESENT YOUR REQUESTS TO GOD

TODAY'S PASSAGE: PHILIPPIANS 4:4–9

Focus verse: Do not be anxious about anything, but in every situation, by prayer and petition, with thanksgiving, present your requests to God.

(Philippians 4:6)

D oes today's passage sound familiar? It's the same one as Day 9. Then we focused on verse four, which tells us to rejoice in the Lord. Today we'll focus on verse six, which tells us to not be anxious about anything and present our requests to God. We do this through prayer.

Regardless of the situation, we pray. Paul says that through prayer and petition, coupled with a thankful heart, we give our requests to God. Let's break this down.

First, Paul tells us not to be anxious about anything. In short, we shouldn't worry. We covered worry in Day 11 when we learned to seek God first. To not be anxious about anything means *anything*—whether big or small, overwhelming or trivial.

In every situation, we turn to God. This starts with prayer and petition.

Though we sometimes view prayer as a petition to God, in a broader sense, prayer is communicating with the Almighty. Through our prayers we worship him. We confess our sins, praise his name, and offer thanksgiving. This is an addition to petitioning him. As a subset of prayer, a petition is to make a specific request to God.

As we make prayers and petitions for every situation, we should come to our Lord with thankful hearts. He made us. He loves us. And he saved us. He also sent us the Holy Spirit. In addition, God gives us many provisions for our lives. As such, we have much to thank God for, but how often do we remember to do this?

With an attitude of thanksgiving, we present our requests to God. Doesn't *presenting our requests to God* sound a lot like petition? It does. It seems Paul wants to make sure we come to God with thankful hearts and not just a list of things we want him to do. Thankfulness is the framework for requesting God's help.

As we pray in every situation, with thanksgiving, we give our anxiousness to Jesus. Therefore, as we move toward a new beginning in our lives, we shouldn't be anxious about it. Instead, we should pray with thankful hearts and give our concerns over to God.

As we do, we can stride forward with expectation and confidence, not in ourselves, but in our Lord.

Questions: *How well do we do at presenting our requests to God in every situation? How often do we remember to thank him for all he's done for us and is still doing?*

Prayer: Jesus, we thank you for loving us and for saving us. We thank you for giving us a new beginning in you and through you. When anxious thoughts assault us, may we give every one of them over to you and wait upon you.

DAY 15: BE RENEWED

TODAY'S PASSAGE: COLOSSIANS 3:5–17

Focus verse: Put on the new self, which is being renewed in knowledge in the image of its Creator. (Colossians 3:10)

In Day 13: Put Off Your Old Self, we talked about moving away from our old self to embrace our new self in Jesus. Paul wrote those instructions to the church in Ephesus. Using similar language, Paul gives the church in Colossae the same directives. Compare today's passage with the one from Day 13: Ephesians 4:17–32.

One difference, however, is Paul's use of the word *renewed* in our focus verse today. He wants us to be renewed.

In considering the verb *renew*, think of a library book. If we haven't finished the book by its due date, we renew it so we can continue reading. We also renew magazine subscriptions, as well as software and service offerings. We take what was and intentionally extend it into the future.

In all these examples, we decide to continue what has already begun. Is this what Paul means when he tells the Colossian church to be renewed? In a way, yes. But renew also means much more. Here's what the dictionary offers us about the word *renew*:

- To make new, as if new again
- To resume
- To reaffirm or repeat
- To restore or revive
- To replenish
- To reestablish
- To extend

The last entry in our list, *extend*, aligns with renewing a library book or subscription. This certainly applies to our faith journey. We might liken it to *re-up*, as in reenlisting for military service. But in this case, we re-up for Jesus—every day.

The other items on our list also give us a deeper understanding of what it means to renew. The first entry, however, carries extra impact. It's like taking something and making it new again.

That's what we do when we follow Jesus as his disciples. Each morning, we renew our commitment to him, as if to make us new again. We are to be renewed in knowledge according to the image of our Creator, which includes Jesus.

We can extend this idea of being renewed in Jesus to being renewed in our new beginnings. Each day we re-up our commitment to move forward with our resolution, goal, or hope for the future.

Neither our faith nor our new beginnings are a one-and-done situation. For both, we must continually renew our commitment.

Questions: *Which definition of* renew *do we most connect with? Just as we renew our faith in Jesus every day, how do we renew our enthusiasm and commitment to move into our new beginning?*

Prayer: Jesus, show us how to renew ourselves in the knowledge of you every day. As we do, may we remember to set aside what was and put on our new self.

DAY 16: CONSIDER IT PURE JOY
TODAY'S PASSAGE: JAMES 1:2–12

Focus verse: Consider it pure joy, my brothers and sisters, whenever you face trials of many kinds.
(James 1:2)

As we embark on the journey into our new beginning, we may envision moving steadfastly toward our anticipated result day by day. We may expect that each day will take us one step closer to reaching our desired outcome, progressing smoothly and without difficulty.

Yet this perspective is both overly optimistic and unrealistic. We should expect to encounter difficulties along the way. These might be hurdles to clear, roadblocks to navigate around, or even closed roads that force us to find a different path.

How should we react when these inevitable problems arise?

Common responses might be frustration, anger, or discouragement. We may want to give up. We may want to cry in frustration.

In Day 10, we talked about crying out for joy. This referred to our unabashed excitement with God and our relationship to him. It was a grand celebration that produced applause and cries of joy.

Yet when we encounter problems that keep us from moving forward to realize what we seek, our impulse to cry is not out of joy, but out of frustration.

But crying in despair isn't the response James wants us to have. Instead, he says to consider it pure joy when we face various trials.

Yes, when the future we hoped for seems to slip from our grasp or disappear from view, we should consider it pure joy.

Why would we do that?

Because we should view this unexpected delay as a test—a test of our faith. The result is that it will produce perseverance. As we persevere, we will mature and become complete. We will lack nothing.

James wraps up this passage by pronouncing blessings on us when we persevere under trial. We endured the test. Then we'll receive the crown of life God has planned for us.

In this life, each time we persevere under trial, we move closer to receiving God's promise for us when our physical life here ends and we join him for eternity.

This is the underlying reason behind our joy— our pure joy—when we face trials of many kinds.

Questions: *What is our reaction when we encounter difficulties along life's journey? Though pure joy may not be our first response when we encounter problems, how can we move to embrace that perspective?*

Prayer: Jesus, show us how to embrace difficulties and disappointments with the pure joy James talks about. May we see how it produces perseverance and helps us become mature and complete, preparing for us to join you in heaven.

DAY 17: GOD CARES FOR US
TODAY'S PASSAGE: 1 PETER 5:6–11

Focus verse: Cast all your anxiety on him because he cares for you. (1 Peter 5:7)

I n Day 14 we looked at Paul's instruction to not be anxious about anything. His prescription to combat worry was prayer (Philippians 4:6).

Peter also tells us to not worry. He writes that we are to cast our anxiety—all of it—on God. We are to give it to him—every bit.

The key is that once we give God our anxieties —our frets for today and our worries about tomorrow—we must not take them back. If we do, it suggests we don't fully trust our Lord to take care of us. May we never make that mistake.

Peter, whose letter overflows with practical teaching, includes other instructions and words of advice in his letter. This passage in particular will help us as we move forward into the new year or to embrace our fresh start.

First, he says we are to humble ourselves before God. Humility prepares us to receive his help when we need it. He'll lift us up in due time. Without humility, we won't depend on him. We'll try to do things on our own. And we will eventually fail.

Next, Peter tells us to cast our anxiety on God because he cares for us. We should turn over to our Heavenly Father all that concerns us. We should give him our worries and not try to bear them alone.

In the next verse, Peter tells us to be alert and sober-minded. We need to watch out for the devil, who seeks to keep us from realizing the outcome we hope for. He prowls. He looks for someone to devour—not physically as much as emotionally and spiritually. Our enemy wants to keep us from realizing what God wants us to have.

We are to resist the devil. We are to stand firm in our faith. In doing so, we should receive consolation, knowing that Jesus's other followers undergo the same struggle.

By God's grace—the same grace that sent Jesus to us—he'll rescue us. He won't let us struggle forever. After we have suffered for a while, God will restore us and make us strong. Through him, we will stand firm and remain steadfast.

For this we give praise to God. We acknowledge his power.

This truth should encourage us as we move forward into our new beginnings.

Questions: *What does it mean that God cares for us? In practical ways, how can we cast all our anxiety on him?*

Prayer: Heavenly Father, may we do as Peter instructs and cast all our anxiety on you. Once we do, may we not take it back, but instead trust you with our future: to restore us and make us strong when the enemy attacks. We ask this in Jesus's name. Amen.

DAY 18: THE DESIRE OF OUR HEARTS
TODAY'S PASSAGE: PSALM 20:1–5

Focus verse: May he give you the desire of your heart and make all your plans succeed. (Psalm 20:4)

The first five verses of Psalm 20 read like a series of uplifting statements from King David to his audience—both then and now. We can receive David's seven godly proclamations as encouragement to us as we move forward to embrace our new beginnings.

Each one begins with the pivotal word *may*. This implies that what follows is both an imperative prayer to our Lord and a proclaimed blessing for us to receive.

1. May God answer your prayers when you're in distress.

We don't need to struggle alone. When difficulties befall us, God will answer our cries for help. All we need to do is ask and wait in expectation for his answer.

2. May God protect you.

The same God that kept Jacob safe did the same for his children, descendants, and the nation he birthed. In this same way, our Lord can—and will—protect us. The Old Testament overflows with accounts of God's provisions, despite his children's many missteps along the way. What God did for them, he'll also do for us.

3. May God send help and grant you support from the sanctuary.

We see God's provisions for us when we're in need. It not only comes from him, but it also comes from his children. In this way, we receive help from others when we need it. We're also encouraged to help them when they need it.

4. May God remember what you've done
   for him.

Though we need to guard against trying to earn God's favor, as aligned with the Old Testament perspective, this can help us remember our relationship with the Almighty. Our right standing with the Father through Jesus is key.

5. May he give you the desire of your heart
   and make your plans succeed.

We must, however, make sure our heart desires what he desires. Our plans must align with his. If we want something contrary to his nature, we shouldn't expect to receive it. Yet when our desires and plans agree with his, we can expect his approval and receive his blessing.

6. May you shout for joy and celebrate
   your victory.

God grants us victory over the opposition that confronts us. We must thank him for it.

7. May God grant all your requests.

This can apply specifically to the first five items on our list and build upon the sixth.

As we move forward to embrace our future, may we seek and receive these blessings from our Heavenly Father.

Questions: *Do we read today's passage more as a prayer or as a proclamation? Which one of the seven items most challenges us? Which one needs our attention the most?*

Prayer: Lord, may we turn these seven items into a heartfelt prayer to you. May we receive their promises as we move forward into our new year or new beginning. Thank you for loving us, caring for us, and watching over us.

DAY 19: WHATEVER WE DO
TODAY'S PASSAGE: COLOSSIANS 3:1–17

Focus verse: Whatever you do, whether in word or deed, do it all in the name of the Lord Jesus, giving thanks to God the Father through him.
(Colossians 3:17)

As we move forward to embrace our future, may we keep our focus on one overall guiding ideal: Whatever we do, we should do it for Jesus. Nothing else matters. Not really.

As we read today's passage, we see repeats of many of the same thoughts we encountered in other days' readings (Day 1: The Old Is Gone and Day 13: Put Off Your Old Self). But let's not look at the repetition as something to skip. Instead, let's embrace it as a reminder of what's essential. May we never tire of hearing about living for Jesus and honoring his Father.

We are to do all things for Jesus, who died to save us and usher us into glory with him. As we do so, we're to put off the old. This means to stop doing the sinful things we used to embrace—often without a second thought.

We should replace them with God-honoring traits: compassion, kindness, humility, gentleness, and patience. We must forgive others as God forgave us through Jesus. And we should do all this through love, which promotes complete unity.

Paul winds down his teaching on how we should live for Jesus with a reminder to let peace guide us, to be thankful, and to encourage fellow believers as we teach and worship with them.

His last instruction is today's focus verse. May all we do—every step of the way—be done for Jesus. This means what we say and what we do. And we're not wrong to expand it to include whatever we think.

We do all things for Jesus. If we chase goals for ourselves, it will mean little. If we pursue achievements for others, it will mean even less.

Other wrong-minded considerations are doing things with greedy intent, to increase our position, or to receive human accolades. When we pursue money, power, and prestige apart from Jesus, we gain nothing of eternal value. And what we may gain of temporal value means little. It may even increase our troubles in life—in fact, it likely will.

As we talk about the new year, as we work toward our goal, and as we think about the future, let us do so in Jesus's name. And may we thank Father God for his provisions through his Son.

Questions: *Do we do things for Jesus, ourselves, or others? How do we make sure our words, actions, and thoughts honor Jesus and respect Papa?*

Prayer: Jesus, as we move into our future, guide us into making sure all we say and do is for your name and for your glory. May we praise our Heavenly Father for all your provisions.

DAY 20: A FUTURE HOPE
TODAY'S PASSAGE: PROVERBS 23:17–18

Focus verse: There is surely a future hope for you, and your hope will not be cut off. (Proverbs 23:18)

The book of Proverbs begins with instructions for Solomon's son. We addressed this in Day 8.

As the book progresses, however, it veers from that purpose and morphs into what often appears to be a series of seemingly random tips of wisdom compiled into a list. As such, there's not much context that surrounds these verses or passages. This is the case with the twenty-third chapter of Proverbs.

Some versions of the Bible group verses 17 and 18 together as a connected thought. Our passage for the day reflects this, and we'll consider them together to inform our journey toward our new beginning as we move forward with Jesus.

Though the climax of this brief passage is the second verse, let's start with the verse that precedes it as a much-needed prelude.

It advises us to avoid envy. Specifically to not let our hearts envy sinners. When we see what others have and want it, this is envy.

It seems worse when those people are sinners. But aren't we all? It's just that we sin to different degrees. Therefore, if everyone is a sinner, we must envy no one. This means to not want what the most defiled person has achieved any more than what the most admirable person has.

Instead of wanting what others have, we should turn our attention to the Lord. We should be zealous in our fear of God. To be zealous is to show enthusiastic devotion. Here, our devotion is to God. We should be more zealous for him than anything else.

Yet our zeal should be in our fear of him. We should not, however, view fear as dread, apprehension, or unpleasant feelings. Instead, we should embrace a secondary meaning of *fear*. It's having extreme reverence and awe.

Therefore, to restate the phrase *be zealous for the fear of the LORD*, we should have an enthusiastic devotion to our Lord, with extreme reverence and awe.

Now that we have set aside envy and enthusiastically given God our extreme awe, we are prepared to move on to the next verse. It's about hope. Because of our Lord, we can hope for a better tomorrow.

This isn't a vague, sentimental wish that our lives will get better. It's a confident expectation that God will provide for us as we intentionally move forward.

This hope in him will not be cut off. We can count on it.

Questions: *How can we move from being envious of others to being zealous for God? Is our hope for our future wishful thinking or confident expectation?*

Prayer: Heavenly Father, guide us as we turn our eyes from what others have and focus on you. May we place our hope in you with confident expectation. We ask this in Jesus's name. Amen.

DAY 21: MY HELPER

TODAY'S PASSAGE: PSALM 118:1–7

Focus verses: The LORD is with me; I will not be afraid. What can mere mortals do to me? The LORD is with me; he is my helper. I look in triumph on my enemies. (Psalm 118:6–7)

The authors of the book of Hebrews wrap up their letter with some final encouragements. Among them is a reminder to say with confidence that God is our helper. Therefore, we have nothing to fear (Hebrews 13:6). This passage, however, comes from the Old Testament, and it's part of today's focus verses.

If God is with us, we should have nothing to fear. Though others may confront us, in our Lord's overall perspective, they can't harm us. At worst, anything they do is temporal. God's protection is eternal. We must keep this in mind when we face fears over the threats and attacks of people. God is greater than them; he is on our side.

To make sure we don't miss it, the writer of the psalm repeats the assurance that God is with him. That same God is also with us.

Let's imagine walking toward our new beginning. Picture Jesus walking at our side. This should fill us with confidence. It should embolden us as we move forward.

As Paul writes to the church in Rome: "If God is for us, who can be against us?" (Romans 8:31).

Next, we read that our Lord is also our helper.

We can seek help from many sources. We can ask our family for assistance and request that friends help us. And we can ask our neighbors. In our job, we can seek support from our coworkers. In other situations, we may summon law enforcement or request relief through the courts. We may even turn to a government official for support.

Yet, in these situations, the help we receive may not be enough. Sometimes it might not help at all. Sometimes the so-called help may even cause us more harm than good.

None of these concerns are true when we turn to God for help. We can rely on him. We can depend on him (Deuteronomy 31:6). He will never let us down.

How do we turn to the Almighty for help? We ask him. This may be a prayer for protection or for guidance on how to best move forward. It could even be a heartfelt plea of "Help!" A prayer to our Lord need not be wordy or eloquent. It merely needs to be sincere.

As we move forward into our new beginning, may we say with confidence that God is with us. Then we'll have no reason to fear. He is our helper.

Questions: *In what ways have we sought God for help in the past? How can we better seek him for help in the future?*

Prayer: Lord Jesus, please walk with us and help us as we move into our new beginnings. Protect us and give us victory. May we put our trust in you and not be afraid.

DAY 22: REMEMBER

TODAY'S PASSAGE: 1 CHRONICLES 16:7–36

Focus verse: Remember the wonders he has done, his miracles, and the judgments he pronounced, you his servants, the descendants of Israel, his chosen ones, the children of Jacob. (1 Chronicles 16:12–13)

When King David has the ark of the Lord brought to Jerusalem, there's much celebration. Afterward, he appoints Asaph and his associates to praise God. We read those words in today's passage.

It's a call to remember what God has done, of his protection through the years. This isn't just to recall God's recent provisions to David, his army, and the nation of Israel. It's also a call to remember what God had done for prior generations.

The response is to praise him, to sing to the Lord, and to give him thanks. He is good, and his love endures forever. They will praise him for all eternity.

Likewise, we will do well to remember all that God has done.

Let's start with the Old Testament. It begins with God creating us and our world. Later God protects Noah and his family during the flood. Next, he leads Abraham into a new land. He guides Isaac and Jacob. Then he keeps Joseph safe through hardships. Four centuries later, the Lord raises up Moses to free his people from captivity and leads them to the land he promised to give them.

Once there, God sends judges to provide relief and kings to lead his people. He protects his prophets when they speak the truth. And he brings his deported people home.

In the New Testament, we see God come to earth as a man through Jesus. God protects his Son from Satan's attacks. This prepares him to heal and to save his people, which extends to us today.

Then God sends the Holy Spirit to guide us in all that we do. He empowers Peter to preach boldly and calls the murderous Saul to turn to him so he can tell others about Jesus.

The Bible records much more about God's protection, provisions, and love for us. We will do well to remember these things.

In addition, we can also remember what he has done to help us personally. We should take time to consider how he has protected us, the provisions he has given, and the many ways his love has overflowed to us. This starts with Jesus dying to save us and restore us into a right relationship with Father God.

Last, consider how God has helped other people too.

For all this, we give him our praise. We look to our Lord and his strength. We seek him in all situations (1 Chronicles 16:11).

As we remember, we receive encouragement as we move into the new year and our new beginnings.

Questions: *What else can we recall from Scripture about God's marvelous wonders? What wonders has he done in our own life that we must remember—and thank him for?*

Prayer: Holy Spirit, when we are discouraged, help us remember all you have done for us and for others. May this encourage us and fill us with confidence to move forward under your power. We ask this in Jesus's name. Amen.

DAY 23: WEAK OR STRONG?

TODAY'S PASSAGE: 2 CORINTHIANS 12:1–10

Focus verse: That is why, for Christ's sake, I delight in weaknesses, in insults, in hardships, in persecutions, in difficulties. For when I am weak, then I am strong. (2 Corinthians 12:10)

I n Paul's second recorded letter to the church in Corinth, he takes time to boast about all he has suffered in service to his Lord (2 Corinthians 11:16–33). It's an inspiring chronicle of endurance that shows his steadfast devotion to doing what God has called him to do—despite opposition and hardship.

In today's passage, Paul continues his boasting of receiving visions from the Lord and going to the third heaven. (Consider the first heaven as our sky, the second heaven as space, and the third heaven as our perception of God's supernatural dwelling place.)

At first, it seems Paul speaks about another person who experienced these things, but as he continues writing, he confirms he is the one who received these visions and revelations from God, as the one who was caught up into the third heaven.

Yet Paul struggled with a prideful attitude over his amazing encounter—something few people experience.

To help keep his conceit in check, he was given a thorn in the flesh—a message from Satan—to afflict him. Though we don't know what this physical disorder was, we know it tormented him greatly.

Three times he pleaded with God to remove it from his body. Though God answered his prayer, it certainly wasn't what Paul expected or wanted. Instead of healing Paul from his infirmity, God allowed the torment to remain, but he did encourage Paul.

The Lord told Paul, "My grace is sufficient for you, for my power is made perfect in weakness."

Therefore, Paul boasted about his weakness because it showed God's power (2 Corinthians 12:9).

As we go forward in life to embrace the new beginning before us, we will do well to seek God for his protection and direction. Yet when God doesn't answer our prayers the way we expect or want, we must not be dismayed or give up. Instead, we should press forward despite not receiving the relief we wanted.

We can confidently agree with Paul that when we are weak, then we are strong.

Questions: *When has God not answered our prayers the way we wanted? How did we respond to this disappointment? When has conceit caused problems? What do we think about being spiritually strong to counter our physical weaknesses?*

Prayer: Jesus, give us your perspective and the strength to be like Paul. When we face hardships, may we not give up but push forward under Holy Spirit power. When we feel weak, may we find our strength in you. So be it.

DAY 24: A HEART AT PEACE
TODAY'S PASSAGE: PROVERBS 14

Focus verse: A heart at peace gives life to the body, but envy rots the bones. (Proverbs 14:30)

Today's focus verse is another wisdom one-liner from the book of Proverbs. It talks about peace.

As we move into the new year, our new beginning, or a fresh start, do we have peace? Peace comes from God. As Paul writes in his letter to the Philippians, God's peace transcends all understanding. It guards our hearts and our minds to maintain our focus on Jesus (Philippians 4:7).

We may not comprehend this God-given peace, but it gives us solace and tranquility. But what if we lack his peace? It suggests something might be amiss.

Perhaps we don't have peace because the direction we're moving misaligns with God's. We may desire something contrary to his will. It may be that we're chasing after a goal we shouldn't pursue. Or it may be that we're selfishly thinking about what's in our own best interest, without giving a thought to what our Lord wants for our life.

To address this, we must align our path forward with what God wants and what will help advance his kingdom.

Another reason we may not have peace is that we're trying to move forward under our own resolve. When we strive to accomplish something using our own power, we're likely to feel stress. Stress is a lack of peace.

This is most true when envy motivates our push forward. We first addressed envy in Day 20, and now we'll build on that discussion. We see what other people have, and we want it for ourselves. Though there's nothing wrong with trying to better ourselves or improve our situation in life, we must do so with the right motives. When we do, we will feel peace.

When envy drives us, it rots our bones. This isn't

in a literal sense, but in a figurative one. Envy eats at us from the inside. It robs us of peace. It produces no joy.

Contrast this to when our heart is full of God's peace. God's peace gives life to our body. Through it, we grow. We blossom. And we honor him.

Questions: *Is our heart at peace? If not, what should we do to realign with God's perspective? Is our body full of life or are we rotting on the inside?*

Prayer: Father God, fill us with your peace that transcends all understanding. Guide us into aligning our perspective with yours. Remove envy and selfish intent from our lives, replacing it with a God-honoring outlook. Thank you.

DAY 25: NEW NAMES

TODAY'S PASSAGE: DANIEL 1:1–20

Focus verse: The chief official gave them new names: to Daniel, the name Belteshazzar; to Hananiah, Shadrach; to Mishael, Meshach; and to Azariah, Abednego. (Daniel 1:7)

King Nebuchadnezzar conquers Jerusalem, raids the temple, and forces many young men of royalty and nobility into service for him. Among them are Daniel, Hananiah, Mishael, and Azariah. The king gives them new names.

This is an effort to strip them of their heritage and diminish their beliefs. Their new Babylonian names reflect their new reality. If the king treats them as Babylonian, he expects they will begin to act Babylonian and eventually accept its ways.

Daniel's new name of Belteshazzar is extra upsetting. It's a nod to the Babylonian god Bel. Being renamed after a foreign god surely distresses this God-fearing lad.

Later, another of the Hebrew captives, Hadassah, receives the Persian name of Esther (Esther 2:7). It's also an attempt to remove her past.

For all five, a foreign power forced unfamiliar names upon them. The intent was to re-orient them, even reprogram them, to accept foreign ways.

Contrast this to when God gives us a new name. Through God, Abram becomes Abraham (Genesis 17:5). Sarai becomes Sarah (Genesis 17:15–16). And Jacob becomes Israel (Genesis 32:28).

These three name changes occur after they experience an encounter with God. He does so to set them on a fresh path and encourage them to expand their perspective. For each one, it marks a new beginning in their lives. When God gives us a new name, he has a good reason.

Let's also look at two instances when people gave themselves a new name.

Consider Ruth's mother-in-law, Naomi. Naomi means pleasant. But, disappointed at the death of her husband and both sons, Naomi asks people to call her Mara, which means bitter (Ruth 1:20). But there's no mention in Scripture that anyone ever does. As we later read in the book of Ruth, God blesses Naomi with a grandson, removing her bitter disappointment and replacing it with immense joy.

Another situation is Saul, also called Paul (Acts 13:9). This is not a name change orchestrated by God or forced upon him by others. Instead, it's likely a means to facilitate ministry. Saul is a Hebrew name, but his ministry is to non-Hebrew people. Paul is a name of Latin origin. As Saul travels the area to minister to non-Jewish people, going by the name of Saul is a potential roadblock to effective ministry, whereas going by Paul removes that concern. In doing so, he reaches many for God.

Names matter—to both us and to God.

Questions: *Does God have a special name for us? Whether or not God gives us a new name, what is he doing to give us a renewed outlook as we move into our future? When others give us a new name, how should we react? When might we want to give ourselves a new name?*

Prayer: Holy Spirit, do you have a new name for us? Regardless, please give us an elevated perspective of your purpose as we move into our future. If people have given us hurtful names, remove the pain and replace it with God-honoring confidence. We ask this in Jesus's name. Amen.

DAY 26: GOD IS FOR US

TODAY'S PASSAGE: ROMANS 8:18–31

Focus verse: If God is for us, who can be against us? (Romans 8:31)

In today's passage, Paul, writing to the church in Rome, discusses their present suffering in contrast to the future glory they'll experience through Jesus. The beginning of this passage is not the type of feel-good message we like to read, but it's an important one to be aware of.

It provides a wise reminder that just because we follow Jesus doesn't guarantee everything will be easy for us. As God's children, we will suffer. We will struggle. This is our reality, but we should not let it dictate our response. In Jesus, we have a rock-solid foundation to place our hope on.

Just as creation has been groaning because of sin's infiltration, we too groan as we wait for what happens next. Through Jesus, we have confidence of being adopted into the Father's sonship and the redemption of our physical bodies. This is our hope, which results from our salvation.

Just as creation groans and we groan, the Holy Spirit helps us when we feel weak. When we struggle to pray, the Holy Spirit intercedes on our behalf with wordless groans. He prays for us.

With this as our foundation, we know God will work out everything for good to those who love him and are called according to his purpose. This isn't, however, a promise that he'll give us everything we want. It's a promise that our Lord will work out every situation for what he views as best overall.

But this promise doesn't apply to everyone. It only applies to those who love him and are called by him, that is, to all followers of Jesus.

Despite the difficulties we may face as we move forward in life, we know three things:

First, the Holy Spirit groans in prayer for us when we don't know how to pray.

Next, we know God will work out everything according to his good purpose.

Third, as today's focus verse says, we know that with God being for us, no one can be against us.

In Day 21, we envisioned Jesus walking next to us as we go about our day. Now let's expand this image. Jesus walks on one side, the Father on the other, and the Holy Spirit hovers over us. God's protection surrounds us wherever we go.

In this way, we see that God is with us, and no one can stand against us.

Questions: *How are we encouraged, knowing that the Holy Spirit prays for us when we don't know what to pray? How do we react when the way God works things out isn't what we wanted? Do we feel God is with us as we go about our day?*

Prayer: Father, Son, and Holy Spirit, we thank you for your promises that we read about in today's passage. May we understand them, accept them, and embrace them as we move forward into our new beginning. Thank you for being with us as we go and protecting us from those who oppose us.

DAY 27: AN UNDIVIDED HEART
TODAY'S PASSAGE: EZEKIEL 11:14–25

Focus verse: "I will give them an undivided heart and put a new spirit in them; I will remove from them their heart of stone and give them a heart of flesh." (Ezekiel 11:19)

In Day 3 we looked at Ezekiel 36:26. In that reading, we talked about God giving us a new heart and a new spirit, about our Lord removing our heart of stone and replacing it with a heart of flesh. We see all these phrases repeated in our focus verse for today. It's a worthy reminder of what matters.

But there's one new phrase for us to consider: an undivided heart.

God promises to give his people an undivided heart. If he promised it to them back then, can we claim that promise today?

Regardless of our answer to this question, we can certainly ask for God to give us an undivided heart. That's exactly what King David does. He prays that the Lord will teach him, that he'd rely on God's faithfulness. Then David requests that the Almighty will give him an undivided heart so that he will fear the Lord's name (Psalm 86:11).

We can make this same request of God today, that he'll give us an undivided heart. But why would we want one?

Jesus teaches that we cannot serve two masters. We will hate the one and love the other (Luke 16:13). In this teaching, Jesus refers to trying to serve both God and money. Yet the impossible task of trying to pursue two conflicting objectives simultaneously is universal; it applies in every situation. Our second master—be it money or some other worldly pursuit—will distract us from serving God. It will pull us away from him.

Therefore, we need an undivided heart as we move forward in life. If we don't have a singular intent as we step into our new beginning, we will divide our focus. As a result, we will probably fail to realize our objectives. We can't have two priorities. We can only have one.

May we make God our priority. Then he can affirm us, just like he did David, as a person after his own heart (Acts 13:22).

This all starts when we ask our Lord to give us an undivided heart.

Questions: *How may our heart be divided today? Who or what are we trying to serve that distracts us from God?*

Prayer: Jesus, give us an undivided heart. When we pick up our cross to follow you, may we not look back to see what we left behind. May we not pursue another master. Give us strength to move steadfastly into our new beginning through you. Amen.

DAY 28: THE HOLY SPIRIT
TODAY'S PASSAGE: ROMANS 5:1–9

Focus verse: God's love has been poured out into our hearts through the Holy Spirit, who has been given to us. (Romans 5:5)

In many of our readings, we talked about the Holy Spirit. As a member of the three-in-one Godhead, we also directed some of our prayers specifically to him. Though this may not be a common practice for everyone, it's a worthy exercise to consider. In doing so, it reminds us that God is three persons in one, comprised of the Father, Son, and Holy Spirit. We can pray to them as a whole or specifically to one part.

In Day 3 we talked about God sending his

followers the Holy Spirit on Pentecost. On that momentous day, the Holy Spirit settled on them like tongues of fire; he gave them supernatural power (Acts 2:1–12). From that day forward, the Holy Spirit lived in Jesus's followers and guided them in everything they did.

As Jesus's followers today, this same Holy Spirit that lived in his disciples then also lives in us. As such, the Holy Spirit is at work in our lives and can help us as we move into our new beginnings.

But not everyone who follows Jesus realizes that the Holy Spirit lives within them. Though he's present, they may not know it. Therefore, we must be open to the Holy Spirit's presence in us and allow him to guide us and to work through us. We can choose to listen to him, or we can choose to ignore him. May we listen and then obey.

This means that as we move into our new beginnings, the Holy Spirit is with us. He can give us assurance when we are unsure. He can give us direction when we don't know which way to turn. And he can give us a supernatural confidence that can only come from God.

We can pray to the Holy Spirit. We can ask him for clarity and seek direction. And we can listen to his still, small voice as we move throughout our day.

Though hearing the Holy Spirit speak to us may be an uncomfortable consideration for some, with practice, we can all learn to hear the Holy Spirit when he talks.

Emboldened by the Holy Spirit, we can move into the new year with confident expectation. As we said in Day 26, if God is with us, who can stand against us? (Romans 8:31).

Questions: *What role does the Holy Spirit play in our lives? How well do we do at obeying him? If we aren't aware of his presence, what can we do to learn more about him?*

Prayer: Holy Spirit, may we depend on you as we move forward into the new year. When you speak to us, may we listen and hear. Give us strength to obey what you say. Guide us in all that we do and give us direction as we journey into our new beginnings. Amen.

DAY 29: RUN WITH PERSEVERANCE
TODAY'S PASSAGE: HEBREWS 12:1–3

Focus verse: Let us run with perseverance the race marked out for us. (Hebrews 12:1)

Whenever we start something new, we overflow with excitement. We look forward to what will be, which fills us with hope. We have a resolve to push forward regardless of what we encounter. At this beginning moment, our expectations and confidence are at their highest.

From this lofty starting point, however, all our encouraging emotions will gradually slip away. Our excitement will wane. Our hopeful anticipation will waver. And our resolve will become not so resolute.

In short, we'll reach a point where we want to give up. The day will surely come when we feel we have nothing left and can't push forward.

We shouldn't be discouraged, however, when this day happens, for it's bound to occur. Instead, we should recognize that our journey forward will one day face a crisis. When we encounter it, we can quit or we can persevere. May we choose to persevere.

Jesus is our primary example of perseverance. He endured the pain of crucifixion and the shame of a criminal's death. He endured opposition. May we remember Jesus's sacrifice when we're weary or lose heart on our journey through life.

The writers of the book of Hebrews likewise encourage their audience to run their race with perseverance. That extends to us today.

But what if we feel we can't?

For inspiration, let's look at the life of Paul. We touched on this briefly in Day 23, when he boasted to the church in Corinth of all he endured so he could tell others about Jesus (2 Corinthians 11:16–33).

In Paul's missionary quest, he was often imprisoned and severely flogged. He was repeatedly exposed to death. Five times he received thirty-nine lashes, three times he was beaten with rods, and once he was stoned. He was shipwrecked three times and spent the night on the open sea. He faced threats from flooding, rivers, and bandits, even from his own people. Paul worked hard, missed sleep, and went hungry. He was sometimes cold and even naked.

Through all this, Paul persevered. Yet he didn't persevere on his own. He persevered by faith and through the strength God gave him. This is key.

When we face opposition as we move into our new beginnings, coupled with our own diminished determination, we shouldn't try to push through on our own. If we attempt this, we will probably fail.

Instead, we should seek our Lord for the strength to carry on. With him, we can persevere to run the race marked out for us. May we do so.

Questions: *How do we normally react when we face difficulties? Is our first inclination to turn to God or to strive forward under our own power? How can the examples of Jesus and Paul encourage us today?*

Prayer: Father God, may we turn to you for strength when we are discouraged. May we persevere as we run the race marked out for us. Let Jesus be our guide and may Paul's example encourage us. Amen.

DAY 30: A NEW BIRTH
TODAY'S PASSAGE: 1 PETER 1:3–9

Focus verse: Praise be to the God and Father of our Lord Jesus Christ! In his great mercy he has given us new birth into a living hope through the resurrection of Jesus Christ from the dead. (1 Peter 1:3)

Throughout our readings, we've often mentioned following Jesus. Though we don't need to be his disciple to embark upon our new beginning, it can help; in fact, it most certainly will. As we move forward to embrace the new year, we can do so with Jesus. His presence in our lives adds meaning and purpose to our quest.

Saying yes to Jesus and following him as his disciple is the most monumental decision we will ever make in our life. He gives us a new birth. In short, we are born again through him (John 3:1–21 and 1 Peter 1:23).

In this life, we will never experience a new beginning more significant than the fresh start we have with Jesus. It's that important.

Our new birth in Jesus gives us a living hope that will last our entire life and usher us into eternity. Jesus conquered death by rising from the dead. When we follow him, we, too, will likewise experience an everlasting life when our earthly body dies. Then we will live with him forever in a new heaven and a new earth.

Compared to our new beginning with Jesus, every other new beginning becomes secondary. We must keep this in mind as we move forward, remembering that our fresh start with Jesus is the one that matters most. Everything else merely adds to it.

Our new birth—that is, our new life—with Jesus becomes the foundation on which we build everything else for the rest of our days. It's a starting point for our new year, our new beginning, and our fresh start.

As we move forward to embrace the future, doing so with Jesus and for Jesus will bolster our excitement, increase our resolve, and focus our attention.

Living life with Jesus doesn't guarantee success, but it certainly increases the potential to realize what we hope for, dream for, and pray for.

May it be so.

Questions: *How does the fact that we're Jesus's followers change our perspective as we move toward our new tomorrow? What can we do to make Jesus a bigger part of our everyday life?*

Prayer: Lord Jesus, thank you for loving us. Thank you for dying in our place for all the wrong things we have done and ever will do. We praise you for rising from the grave, proving your mastery over death. We look forward to spending every day with you, both in this world and the next. Thank you, Jesus!

If you're still on the fence about following Jesus, don't wait another day. Now is the time to make the most important decision of your life. Say "yes" to Jesus today. See Romans 10:9–10.

DAY 31: MAKE EVERYTHING NEW
TODAY'S PASSAGE: REVELATION 21:1–8

Focus verse: He who was seated on the throne said, "I am making everything new!" (Revelation 21:5)

In Day 30 we said our decision to follow Jesus was the most monumental one we could ever make. Through him we experience a new life. Our new life in Jesus is the framework from which all our other new beginnings spring—every one of them.

May we keep Jesus forefront in our mind as we move into the new year, our new beginning, or our fresh start in life. He should be the underlying reason why we do anything and everything. All we do every day should honor him and celebrate the new life he gives us.

Yet we can anticipate one more new thing in our future. As Jesus's followers, when we die, we will live with him for eternity in the new heaven and the new earth that God will make for us at the end of time.

From his heavenly throne, Father God says, "I'm making everything new."

This will mark the final new beginning for us. It will be the ultimate new experience.

Unlike the struggles we face on earth as we seek to move into the new year, in heaven, all struggles will cease. Strife and stress will be no more. We will encounter no enemies to confront us, no walls to keep us out, and no obstacles to hurdle. It will be an idyllic paradise.

May we keep this future outcome in mind as we move forward with our day-to-day effort in embracing our new beginnings here on earth.

As we do so, may all we do bring honor to Jesus, point others to him, and grow his kingdom. This is our purpose in life and the highest goal we can pursue.

Likewise, as we move forward in our new life with Jesus, let us remember our ultimate destination is with him and the Father in heaven. May all we do now be done in anticipation of what will happen then, after we die.

Questions: *How can we be more effective at living every day for Jesus? How should the anticipation of our future home in heaven reflect our attitudes and actions today?*

Prayer: Jesus, through you we have eternal life. Thank you! May we be always mindful that this eternal life started the day we said yes to you. Let it frame all we do here on earth. May we also look beyond our physical time here in this world to a never-ending future with you in heaven. What a glorious day that will be!

If you liked *New Year with Jesus*, please leave a review online. Your review will help others discover this book and encourage them to read it too.

Thank you.

HOLIDAY CELEBRATION DEVOTIONALS

Which devotional do you want to read next?

- *The Advent of Jesus*
- *The Passion of Jesus* (Lent)
- *The Victory of Jesus* (Easter)
- *The Ministry of Jesus*
- *Thanksgiving with Jesus*

Be the first to hear about Peter's new books and receive updates at PeterDeHaan.com/updates.

IF YOU'RE NEW TO THE BIBLE

Each entry in this book contains Bible references. These can guide you if you want to learn more. If you're not familiar with the Bible, here's an overview to get you started, give some context, and minimize confusion.

First, the Bible is a collection of works written by various authors over several centuries. Think of the Bible as a diverse anthology of godly communication. It contains historical accounts, poetry, songs, letters of instruction and encouragement, messages from God sent through his representatives, and prophecies.

Most versions of the Bible have sixty-six books grouped into two sections: The Old Testament and the New Testament. The Old Testament contains thirty-nine books that precede and anticipate Jesus. The New Testament includes twenty-seven books and covers Jesus's life and the work of his followers.

The reference notations in the Bible, such as Romans 3:23, are analogous to line numbers in a Shakespearean play. They serve as a study aid. Since the Bible is much longer and more complex than a play, its reference notations are more involved.

As already mentioned, the Bible is an amalgam of books, or sections, such as Genesis, Psalms, or Matthew. These are the names given to them, over time, based on the piece's author, audience, or purpose.

In the 1200s, each book was divided into chapters, such as Acts 2 or Psalm 23. In the 1500s, the chapters were further subdivided into verses, such as John 3:16. Let's use this as an example.

The name of the book (John) appears first, followed by the chapter number (3), a colon, and then the verse number (16). Sometimes called a chapter-verse reference notation, this helps people quickly find a specific text regardless of their version of the Bible.

Although the goal was to place these chapter and verse divisions at logical breaks, they sometimes seem arbitrary. Therefore, it's good practice to read what precedes and follows each passage you're studying. The text before or after it may contain relevant insights into the portion you're exploring.

Here's how to look up a specific passage in the Bible based on its reference: Most Bibles contain a table of contents, which gives the page number for the beginning of each book. Start there. Locate the book you want to read, and turn to that page. Then flip forward to the chapter you want. Last, skim that chapter to locate the specific verse.

If you want to read online, enter the reference into BibleGateway.com or BibleHub.com. Also check out the YouVersion Bible App.

Learn more about the greatest book ever written at ABibleADay.com, which provides a Bible blog, summaries of the books of the Bible, a dictionary of Bible terms, Bible reading plans, and other resources.

ABOUT PETER DEHAAN

Peter DeHaan, PhD, wants to change the world one word at a time. His books and blog posts discuss God, the Bible, and church, geared toward spiritual seekers and church dropouts. Many people feel church has let them down, and Peter seeks to encourage them as they search for a place to belong.

But he's not afraid to ask tough questions or make religious people squirm. He's not trying to be provocative. Instead, he seeks truth, even if it makes people uncomfortable. Peter urges Christians to push past the status quo and reexamine how they practice their faith in every part of their lives.

Peter earned his doctorate, awarded with high distinction, from Trinity College of the Bible and Theological Seminary. He lives with his wife in beautiful Southwest Michigan and wrangles crossword puzzles in his spare time.

A lifelong student of Scripture, Peter wrote the 1,000-page website ABibleADay.com to encourage people to explore the Bible, the greatest book ever written. His popular blog, at PeterDeHaan.com, addresses biblical Christianity to build a faith that matters.

Read his blog, receive his newsletter, and learn more at PeterDeHaan.com.

BOOKS BY PETER DEHAAN

Holiday Celebration Devotionals

The Advent of Jesus

The Passion of Jesus (Lent)

The Victory of Jesus (Easter)

The Ministry of Jesus

Thanksgiving with Jesus

New Year with Jesus

40-Day Bible Study Series

Dear Theophilus (the Gospel of Luke)

Acts Bible Study

Isaiah Bible Study

Minor Prophets Bible Study

Job Bible Study

Living Water (John)

Love Is Patient (1 and 2 Corinthians)

Revelation Bible Study

1, 2, & 3 John Bible Study

Hebrews Bible Study

James and Jude Bible Study

Matthew Bible Study

1 & 2 Peter Bible Study

Mark Bible Study

Bible Character Sketches Series

Women of the Bible

The Friends and Foes of Jesus

Old Testament Sinners and Saints

More Old Testament Sinners and Saints

Heroes and Heavies of the Apocrypha

200 Old Testament Sinners and Saints

Visiting Churches Series

52 Churches

The 52 Churches Workbook

More Than 52 Churches

The More Than 52 Churches Workbook

Visiting Online Church

Other Books

Elephant God

Jesus's Broken Church

Martin Luther's 95 Theses

The Christian Church's LGBTQ Failure

Bridging the Sacred-Secular Divide (formerly *Woodpecker Wars*)

Beyond Psalm 150

For the latest list of all Peter's books, go to PeterDeHaan.com/nonfiction.